STARTERS

Chocolate

Saviour Pirotta

A+

First published by Hodder Wayland
338 Euston Road, London NW1 3BH, United Kingdom
Hodder Wayland is an imprint of Hodder Children's
Books, a division of Hodder Headline Limited.

This edition published under license from Hodder
Children's Books. All rights reserved.
Text copyright © Saviour Pirotta 2003

Design: Perry Tate Design, Language consultant: Andrew Burrell,
Consultant: Dr. Carol Ballard

Published in the United States by Smart Apple Media
1980 Lookout Drive, North Mankato, MN 56003

Library of Congress Cataloging-in-Publication Data

Pirotta, Saviour.
Chocolate / by Saviour Pirotta. p. cm. — (Starters)
Contents: Yummy chocolate — All sorts of chocolate — Chocolate trees — Get those
pods — Beans, beans everywhere — The chocolate factory — Cocoa butter, cocoa
powder — Making chocolate — Ready at last — Choccy chocolate.
ISBN 1-58340-264-0 1. Chocolate—Juvenile literature. 2. Cookery (Chocolate).
[1. Chocolate.] I. Title. II. Series.
TX817.C4P57 2003 641.3'374—dc21   2003042489

9 8 7 6 5 4 3 2 1

The publishers would like to thank the following for permission to reproduce
photographs in this book: Anthony Blake Library; cover, title page, contents page, 4,
6 (bottom), 8, 13, 14, 17, 20, 22, 23 (left), 24 (top and fourth from top) / Cephas; 5, 9,
10 (top), 11, 12, 19, 24 (bottom) / Corbis; 6 (top), 7, 10 (bottom), 16, 24 (second and
third from top) / Dorling Kindersley Images; 15 / Cadburys; 18 / Food Features; 21

Contents

Wonderful chocolate 4

All kinds of chocolate 6

Chocolate trees 8

Harvesting pods 10

Beans everywhere 12

The chocolate factory 14

Cocoa butter and powder 16

Making chocolate 18

Ready at last 20

Delicious chocolate! 22

Glossary and index 24

Wonderful chocolate

Chocolate is delicious! There is dark chocolate, milk chocolate, and white chocolate.

Chocolate comes in all shapes and sizes. You can buy chocolate bars, chocolate eggs, chocolate syrup, and chocolate chips.

Some chocolate bars are very big.

Chocolate chips are very small.

All kinds of chocolate

There are many ways to enjoy chocolate. Chew it. Drink it. Lick it off your sticky fingers!

Chocolate cake is soft and gooey.

Nothing warms you up like a cup of hot chocolate when it's cold. Nothing cools you down like chocolate ice cream when it's hot.

Chocolate ice cream melts in your mouth.

Chocolate trees

Chocolate is made from the beans of cacao trees. The trees grow in hot countries where it also rains a lot.

HUGE pods grOW on the cacao trees, either on the branches or on the trunk itself.

Inside the pods is a sticky pulp. And hidden in the pulp are lots of beans. They are called cocoa beans.

A pod can have as many as 50 beans inside it. That's enough to make more chocolate than you can eat at one time!

Harvesting pods

When the pods are ripe, farmers cut them down. They use poles with **large** hooks to reach the pods at the tops of trees.

Pods turn orange or red when they're ready to be picked.

The farmers crack the pods open with knives. They scoop out the pulp with the beans inside it.

Piles of pulp and beans are left outside for a few days. The heat from the sun turns the beans deep brown and gives them a nice chocolate flavor.

When the beans turn a rich, chocolate brown, they are picked out of the pulp.

The farmers **spread** them out on mats, tables, and the roofs of their houses to dry in the sun.

Cocoa beans need a lot of warmth to dry.

At last the beans are dry. They are packed into sacks and sent to chocolate factories all over the world.

These beans are ready to be turned into chocolate.

The chocolate factory

At the chocolate factory, the beans are cleaned to make sure there is no dirt left on them. Then they are roasted in huge, hot ovens. This gives them a strong chocolate smell.

These beans have been roasted and are now cooling.

Next, the shells are cracked open so that only the insides are left.

The insides of the beans are called "nibs."

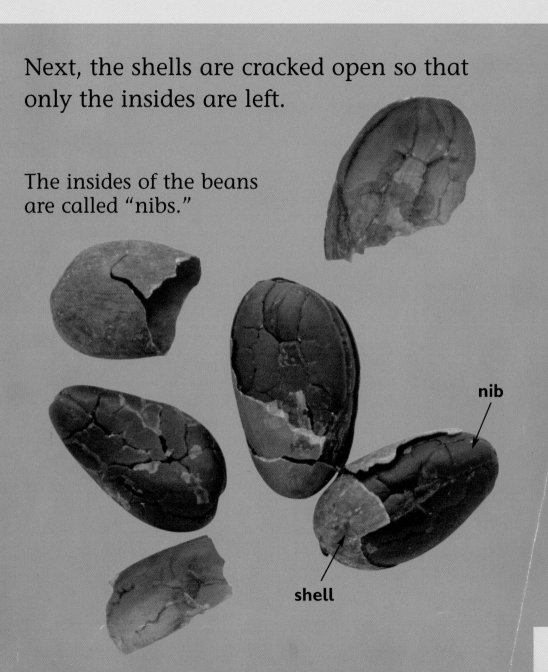

nib

shell

Cocoa butter and powder

The nibs are ground into a thick, dark paste called "cocoa mass." Then the paste is SQUEEZED until it turns into cocoa butter and cocoa powder.

Cocoa butter makes chocolate melt in your mouth.

Cocoa powder can be used to make chocolate drinks and cakes.

Chocolate makers put cocoa mass into a GIANT mixer. They add cocoa butter, milk, and sugar.

The mixer goes around and around until all the ingredients are mixed together.

Steel rollers
then crush the
mixture until
it's nice and
smooth.

Making chocolate
takes a long time.

Ready at last

At last the chocolate makers taste the chocolate. Mmmm. It tastes just right. It's time to pour it into molds and wait until it sets.

The warm chocolate will soon set.

Soon the chocolate will be in stores, ready for you to buy.

Chocolate is one of the most popular foods in the world.

Delicious chocolate!

You can buy chocolate eggs for Easter, chocolate santas for Christmas, and heart-shaped chocolates for Valentine's Day.

Chocolate helps us celebrate in a tasty way!

Glossary and index

Cacao trees Trees that produce the beans from which chocolate is made. **8**

Cocoa beans Seeds that grow on the cacao tree. **9, 11-15**

Cocoa butter The butter-like mush that comes out of ground cocoa beans. **16**

Cocoa mass A soft, creamy paste that forms when cocoa nibs are crushed. **16, 18**

Cocoa powder The powder that's left behind when cocoa butter is taken out of cocoa beans. **16-17**

Nibs The hard centers of cocoa beans. **15-16**

Pods Seed-containing shells that grow on trees and plants. **8-11**

Pulp Mushy material that protects the seeds in a pod. **11-12**